Retire Wealthy, Live Happily

The Ultimate Guide to Financial Freedom in Retirement

By

Bertha C. kein

Copyright © 2024 by Bertha C. kein

All rights reserved. No part of this publication may be reproduced, distributed, or transmitted in any form or by any means, including photocopying, recording, or other electronic or mechanical methods, without the prior written permission of the publisher, except in the case of brief quotations embodied in critical reviews and certain other noncommercial uses permitted by copyright law.

Table of content

Introduction
Chapter 1:
Assessing Your Current Financial Situation
    I: Calculating Net Worth
    II: Evaluating Assets and Liabilities
    III: Analyzing Cash Flow
Chapter2:
Creating a Budget for Retirement Success
    I: Essentials of Budgeting
    II: Setting Realistic Spending Limits.
    III: Strategies for Cutting Costs and Saving More
Chapter 3:
Strategies for Debt-Free Retirement
    I: Identifying and Managing Debt
    II: Paying Off High-Interest Debts
Chapter 4:
Understanding Retirement Accounts and Investment Options.
    I: Overview of Retirement
    II: Selecting the Right Investment Vehicles
    III: Diversification and Risk Management

Chapter 5:
Maximizing Retirement Contribution and Employer Benefits
    I: Strategies to Maximize Contributions
    II: Making Use of Employer Matches and Benefits
    III: Identifying Additional Savings Opportunities

Chapter 6:
Investing for Long-Term Growth and Stability
    I: Principles of Long-Term Investment
    II: Create a Balanced Investment Portfolio
    III: Managing and adjusting your investments over time

Chapter 7:
Decoding Social Security and Pension Benefits
    I: Understanding Social Security Benefits.
    I: Maximizing Your Social Security Income.
    III: Understanding Pension Plans and Benefits.

Chapter 8:
Health and Long-Term Care Planning for Retirement
    II: Long-term Care Insurance Options.
    III: Strategies to Maintain Health and Wellness

Chapter 9:
Estate Planning and Legacy Building.
    I: The importance of estate planning.
    II: Creating a Will and Trust
    III: Preserving Your Legacy for Future Generations

Chapter 10:

Managing Retirement Transitions and Lifestyle Changes
    I: Accepting Retirement Transitions.
    II: Adjusting Financial Strategies.
    III: Prioritising Health and Wellness.

Chapter 11:
Accepting Purpose and Meaning in Retirement
    I: Finding Your Retirement Purpose
    II: Staying Engaged and Active.
    III: Making a Lasting Legacy

Chapter 12:
Developing Social Connections and Relationships During Retirement
    I: The Value of Social Connections
    II: Creating Meaningful Relationships
    III: Developing Existing Relationships.

Conclusion:

Introduction

In a world where uncertainty reigns and the future often appears to be a distant mirage, there is one unavoidable truth that we must all face: retirement. It is a chapter of life we eagerly await but frequently overlook in the midst of our daily grind. Retirement is more than just a milestone; it is a journey that necessitates careful planning, unwavering dedication, and unwavering commitment. Despite the complexities and uncertainties, there is a ray of hope,a road map to financial independence and happiness in retirement.

Consider a life in which your golden years are truly golden, where financial worries are a distant memory, and every day is filled with joy, purpose, and fulfillment. This is not just a dream; it is a tangible reality that is within your reach. **"Retire Wealthy, Live Happily:** *The Ultimate Guide to*

Financial Freedom in Retirement" is more than just a book; it is your ticket to a prosperous and satisfying future.

As you hold this book, you are about to embark on a journey that will change your perspective on retirement and empower you to take control of your financial future. But why should you put your time, money, and trust in this guidebook?

First and foremost, the stakes could not be higher. The decisions you make today will have an impact on the rest of your life and the quality of your retirement. Whether you are just starting out or nearing the end of your career, now is the time to take action. Every moment lost is an opportunity to secure a better future for yourself and your loved ones.

Second, the wisdom contained within these pages is not theoretical; it has been distilled from decades of research, real-world experience, and tried-and-true success strategies. There will be no empty promises or get-rich-quick schemes here, just practical advice, actionable insights, and time-tested principles that have stood the test of time.

Perhaps most importantly, because you deserve it. You have worked tirelessly, made endless sacrifices, and overcome numerous challenges to get to this point in your life. Do not let fear or uncertainty prevent you from enjoying the retirement you have always desired. You can retire wealthy and live happily ever after with the right guidance, mindset, and plan in place.

So, as you embark on this journey, keep in mind that the road to retirement may be long and winding, but with the right map in hand, each step brings you closer to a future filled with abundance, fulfillment, and happiness. **Welcome to "Retire Wealthy, Live Happily,"** where the best days are yet to come.

Chapter 1:

Assessing Your Current Financial Situation

We embark on a critical journey toward safeguarding your financial future: an assessment of your current financial position. This step is critical, regardless of age or life stage, as it serves as the foundation for effective retirement planning. By carefully assessing your financial situation, you gain invaluable insights that will inform and guide your path to retirement readiness.

I: Calculating Net Worth

Net worth provides a complete picture of your financial situation, including all of your assets and liabilities. Make a detailed list of your assets, including cash, investments, retirement accounts, real estate, and personal property, to determine your net worth. Identify and document your liabilities, which may include mortgages, loans, credit card debts, and other financial obligations. After you have calculated these figures, subtract your total liabilities from your total assets. The result is your net worth.

This exercise clarifies your financial situation, revealing whether your assets outweigh your debts or if changes are required to achieve a more favorable balance. It also serves as a tangible indicator of your financial health by providing a baseline for measuring financial progress over time.

II: Evaluating Assets and Liabilities

Examine each asset and liability separately to gain a better understanding of your financial situation. Sort your assets into categories based on liquidity, longevity, and growth potential. Cash and cash equivalents provide immediate liquidity, whereas investments in stocks, bonds, and mutual funds provide long-term growth potential. Real estate investments may provide both appreciation and rental income. Evaluate each asset's performance, consider its contribution to your overall financial strategy, and ensure it aligns with your retirement plans.

Analyze your liabilities to identify areas of concern or potential for improvement. Prioritize debts based on their interest rates, repayment terms, and other requirements. Mortgages, student loans, and credit card balances may have different interest rates and repayment terms, affecting your financial flexibility and long-term solvency. Create a plan to manage and reduce liabilities, with a focus on high-interest debts and debt consolidation strategies to simplify repayment and reduce interest costs.

III: Analyzing Cash Flow

Understanding your cash flow dynamics is essential for sound financial management and retirement planning. Cash flow analysis entails examining your income sources, expenses, and spending habits to determine your financial viability and identify areas for improvement. Begin by recording all sources of income, including salaries, bonuses, investment dividends, rental income, and other cash inflows.

Next, Divide your expenses into fixed and variable categories, including basics like housing, utilities, transportation, groceries, healthcare, and discretionary spending on entertainment, dining, travel, and leisure activities. Analyze your spending habits to see where you may cut back or reallocate funds for savings and investing.

Furthermore, consider the stability and durability of your income streams, as well as their potential to support your chosen lifestyle in retirement. Consider extra income-generating possibilities, such as part-time work, freelance engagements, or passive income sources, to complement your retirement savings and improve financial stability.

Reviewing your existing financial condition prepares you for informed decision-making and strategic planning as you begin your retirement journey. Gaining clarity on your net worth, evaluating your assets and obligations, and analyzing your cash flow dynamics enables you to proactively manage financial issues, capitalize on opportunities, and ultimately achieve your retirement goals with confidence and assurance.

Chapter 2:

Creating a Budget for Retirement Success

We will discuss how to create a budget tailored to your retirement goals. A well-designed budget, regardless of age or financial ability, is the foundation of sound financial management and long-term planning. Setting clear spending limits and matching your expenses to your income and retirement goals can help you have a secure and enjoyable retirement.

I: Essentials of Budgeting

Budgeting is the process of arranging your financial resources to fulfill your immediate and future requirements while also reaching your long-term financial goals. Start by calculating your overall income, which includes salary, bonuses, investment dividends, rental income, and any other sources of cash. Next, divide your spending into fixed and variable categories, distinguishing between essentials.

Set realistic spending limitations for each category based on your financial situation and retirement goals. Aim to achieve a balance between living comfortably today and saving for tomorrow's needs. Use budgeting tools and software to simplify the process and track your progress over time, changing your budget as circumstances and priorities change.

II: Setting Realistic Spending Limits.

Setting realistic spending limitations based on your financial priorities and constraints is a core tenet of good budgeting. Prioritize necessary living expenditures such as housing, utilities, transportation, groceries, healthcare, and insurance premiums, and make certain that these commitments are met consistently and responsibly.

Allow for discretionary spending on non-essential expenses such as dining out, entertainment, travel, and leisure activities, but exercise caution and moderation to avoid overspending and jeopardizing your long-term financial security. Be wary of impulse expenditures and lifestyle inflation, which can deplete your resources and jeopardize your retirement plans over time.

III: Strategies for Cutting Costs and Saving More

Determine how to reduce expenditures and optimize your budget in order to maximize savings and investment contributions. Investigate cost-cutting options in a wide range of spending areas, such as refinancing loans to decrease interest rates, obtaining reductions on recurring payments, and merging insurance policies to save money.

Make lifestyle adjustments and embrace thrifty habits to cut back on needless expenses and divert income towards your retirement savings objectives. Adopt a minimalist attitude that prioritizes experiences above material belongings and recognises the value of mindful consumption. Use technology and automation to simplify financial transactions and savings contributions while maintaining budget consistency and discipline.

Developing a budget for retirement success requires discipline, effort, and strategic planning. Establishing clear spending guidelines, setting realistic limitations, and discovering cost-cutting and savings possibilities can help you attain financial stability and meet your retirement objectives. Remember that a well-crafted budget is not a limitation on your lifestyle, but rather a road map to financial independence and peace of mind in retirement.

Chapter 3:

Strategies for Debt-Free Retirement

Regardless of your age or financial circumstances, good debt management is critical for establishing a strong financial foundation and ensuring your long-term financial well-being. Implementing smart debt management solutions can help you minimize financial stress, increase asset building up, and prepare for a more secure and happy retirement

I: Identifying and Managing Debt

The first stage in debt management is to identify and categorize your loans based on category, interest rates, and payback terms. Common kinds of debt include mortgages, school loans, credit card debt, vehicle loans, and personal loans. Assess each debt's influence on your overall financial health, prioritizing high-interest loans with the potential to deplete your savings and impede your retirement plans.

Once you've identified your obligations, create a detailed debt payback plan that is in line with your financial capabilities and objectives. Consider adopting debt snowball or debt avalanche tactics to gradually pay off debts, focusing on one obligation at a time while making minimum payments on others. Consider refinancing or consolidating high-interest debts to get better terms and reduce monthly payments.

II: Paying Off High-Interest Debts

High-interest debt, such as credit card debt, can be especially harmful to your financial health because of compounding interest and long-term repayment consequences. Prioritize aggressively paying off high-interest loans, devoting greater cash to principal payments to reduce debt and interest charges.

Consider using windfalls, such as tax returns, bonuses, or inheritance, to make lump-sum debt payments and speed up your debt repayment schedule. Additionally, look into balance transfer alternatives or negotiate with creditors to lower interest rates and speed up debt payback. Eliminating high-interest debt early in your financial path allows you to free up resources for retirement savings and investments.

III: Strategies for Debt Consolidation

Debt consolidation is an effective way to streamline debt repayment and simplify your financial obligations. Reduce various loans into a single loan with a lower interest rate or better terms, which reduces the difficulty of handling multiple payments and may result in cheaper overall monthly payments.

Consider consolidation alternatives including personal loans, home equity loans, and balance transfer credit cards to find the best cost-effective solution for your specific financial position. Be aware of the potential costs, fines, and eligibility requirements involved with debt consolidation solutions, and seek expert assistance if necessary to efficiently manage the process.

Efficient debt management is critical for reaching debt-free retirement and establishing a stable financial basis for the future. You may take charge of your financial future and prepare for a more secure and profitable retirement by recognising and prioritizing debt repayment, aggressively paying off high-interest debt, and researching debt consolidation possibilities. Remember that every step towards debt relief takes you closer to financial independence and peace of mind in retirement.

Chapter 4:

Understanding Retirement Accounts and Investment Options.

In this important chapter, we'll look at retirement accounts and investing alternatives, both of which are critical components of a successful retirement strategy. Understanding the different retirement vehicles accessible to you and the investing possibilities they provide is critical to developing a solid financial strategy that will support you throughout your retirement years. By being aware of these possibilities, you will be able to make educated judgments that are consistent with your future objectives and aspirations.

I: Overview of Retirement

Retirement accounts, such as 401(k), Individual Retirement Accounts (IRAs), and Roth IRAs, are effective ways to save and invest for retirement. Each type of account offers various tax advantages, contribution restrictions, and withdrawal rules, allowing flexibility and diversity in your retirement saving strategy

Explore the characteristics and benefits of each retirement account choice, taking into consideration employer contributions, tax-deferred growth, and fund accessibility. Determine which accounts are accessible to you based on your job status, income level, and eligibility conditions, and then prioritize your contributions to maximize tax advantages and investment development opportunities.

II: Selecting the Right Investment Vehicles

After you've established your retirement accounts, the next step is to choose the right investment vehicles to fill them. From equities and bonds to mutual funds, exchange-traded funds (ETFs), and target-date funds, there are several investing alternatives available to meet your risk tolerance, time horizon, and financial

Evaluate the investing possibilities available in your retirement accounts, taking into account asset allocation, diversification, and expense ratios. Create a well-balanced investment portfolio that is consistent with your investing plan, mixing several asset classes to reduce risk and maximize long-term profits.

III: Diversification and Risk Management

Diversification is a key element of cautious investing that reduces portfolio volatility and protects cash in difficult market situations. Diversify your assets across asset classes, sectors, and geographic locations to reduce concentration risk and increase portfolio resilience.

In addition, use risk management tactics like asset allocation, rebalancing, and dollar-cost averaging to reduce downside risk and capitalize on market opportunities. Regularly assess and change your investment portfolio to be in line with your risk tolerance, investing goals, and changing market circumstances, guaranteeing a disciplined and strategic approach to wealth building and preservation.

Understanding retirement accounts and investment alternatives is critical for establishing a sound financial foundation and meeting your retirement objectives. By becoming acquainted with the features and benefits of various retirement accounts, selecting appropriate investment vehicles, and implementing diversification and risk management strategies, you can optimize your investment portfolio and position yourself for a secure and prosperous retirement. Remember, the key to effective investment is knowledge, discipline, and a long-term outlook.

Chapter 5:

Maximizing Retirement Contribution and Employer Benefits

We'll look at how to maximize your retirement contributions and take advantage of company advantages to help you get to a comfortable and happy retirement. Understanding the various retirement savings options and utilizing employer-sponsored programmes may considerably improve your financial well-being in retirement. By increasing your contributions and taking full use of workplace perks, you may maximize tax breaks, increase your savings potential, and create the framework for a happy and joyful retirement.

I: Strategies to Maximize Contributions

Maximizing retirement contributions is critical for creating a substantial nest fund that will last throughout your retirement years. Take full advantage of contribution restrictions established by retirement account providers, such as 401(k) plans and IRAs, to maximize tax-deferred growth potential and speed up wealth building.

Contribute as much as you can to your retirement accounts, aiming to reach or surpass the yearly contribution limits to maximize tax savings and investment growth potential. Consider progressively raising your contribution rate over time, using income rises, bonuses, or windfalls to enhance savings, and capitalizing on compounding interest to maximize long-term profits.

II: Making Use of Employer Matches and Benefits

company-sponsored retirement plans frequently feature useful perks like company matching and profit-sharing contributions, which can greatly increase your retirement savings potential. Contribute enough to your retirement plan to qualify for your employer's maximum matching contribution

To augment your retirement funds and maximize tax advantages, consider extra employment perks such as profit-sharing contributions, employee stock purchase schemes, and deferred pay arrangements. Proactively comprehend and optimize your employer's benefits package, working with human resources or financial experts to examine all available possibilities and maximize your financial rewards.

III: Identifying Additional Savings Opportunities

In addition to employer-sponsored retirement plans, look into other ways to boost your retirement savings and diversify your strategy. Consider creating supplementary retirement accounts, such as Roth or regular IRAs, to supplement employer-sponsored plans and take advantage of tax breaks and investment options.Investigate different savings options, such as health.

Consider alternate savings vehicles, such as health savings accounts (HSAs), education savings accounts (ESAs), or brokerage accounts, to diversify your investment portfolio and take advantage of additional tax benefits. Evaluate your financial objectives and risk tolerance to discover the best savings vehicles and contribution methods for your specific situation.

Maximizing retirement contributions and using employment perks are critical steps towards a safe and profitable retirement. You may speed up asset growth, reduce tax costs, and establish the groundwork for a comfortable and joyful retirement by optimizing your contributions, taking full advantage of employment matching and perks, and exploring other savings possibilities. Remember that the key to retirement success is early planning, disciplined saving, and judicious use of existing resources.

Chapter 6:

Investing for Long-Term Growth and Stability

This section discusses the fundamentals of investing for long-term growth and stability, which are critical for developing a strong financial portfolio that will last throughout your retirement. Understanding the foundations of long-term investing and following a disciplined investment approach will allow you to capitalize on market opportunities, reduce risk, and confidently accomplish your retirement goals.

I: Principles of Long-Term Investment

Long-term investing is predicated on the idea that capital appreciation will occur over a long period of time, generally several decades. Unlike short-term trading, which focuses on market swings and short-lived trends, long-term investment prioritizes basic analysis, strategic asset allocation, and patience.

Create a clear investing strategy based on your financial objectives, risk tolerance, and time timeline, and ensure that your investment decisions are in line with your long-term goals. Adopt a diversified portfolio approach, spreading your assets across several asset classes, sectors, and geographical locations to minimize risk and maximize returns over time.

II: Create a Balanced Investment Portfolio

A well-balanced investment portfolio is critical for long-term growth and security in your retirement resources. Create a diversified portfolio with a combination of stocks, bonds, cash equivalents, and other investments based on your risk tolerance and investing goals.

To maximize diversity and reduce volatility, systematically allocate assets within your portfolio, taking into account aspects such as risk, return potential, and correlation. Rebalance your portfolio on a regular basis to keep it in line with your intended asset allocation and to account for changing market circumstances or life events.

III: Managing and adjusting your investments over time

Monitoring and altering your assets over time is critical for adapting to changing market conditions and staying on pace to achieve your retirement goals. Regularly examine your investment portfolio, analyzing performance measures and determining the suitability of your investments in light of changing economic conditions, market trends, and personal circumstances.

Implement a disciplined approach to investment decision-making, avoiding emotional reactions to short-term market changes while being committed to your long-term investment goal. Consult a financial advisor or investment specialist to learn about market trends, investment possibilities, and portfolio optimisation.

Investing for long-term growth and stability is critical for developing a strong financial portfolio and meeting your retirement objectives. Understanding the concepts of long-term investing, creating a balanced investment portfolio, and monitoring and changing your investments over time may help you capitalize on market opportunities, reduce risk, and assure a bright future. Remember that effective investment needs patience, discipline, and a long-term outlook.

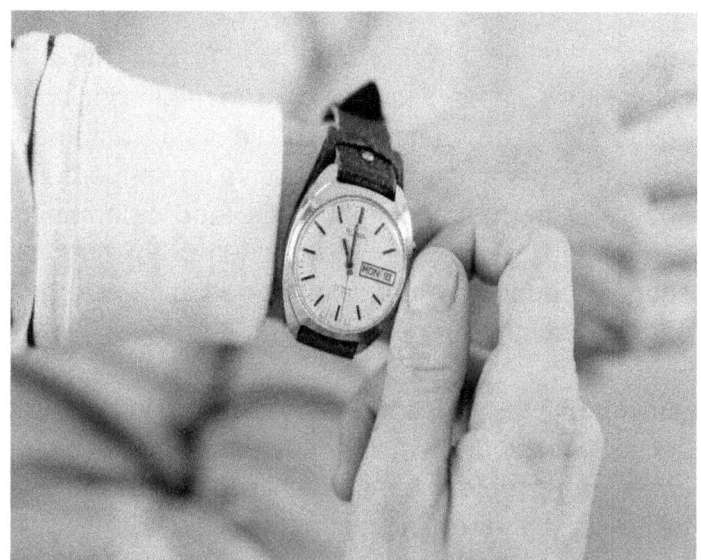

Chapter 7:

Decoding Social Security and Pension Benefits

There are intricacies of Social stability and pension benefits, two sources of retirement income that can have a considerable influence on your financial stability in retirement. Understanding how these benefits function, when to claim them, and how they fit into your overall retirement strategy is critical to maximizing your income and ensuring a happy retirement

I: Understanding Social Security Benefits.

Social Security is a government programme that provides cash assistance to qualified persons during retirement, disability, and survivorship. To be eligible for Social Security benefits, you must have earned a sufficient number of work credits through Social Security-tax-paying employment.

Learn how Social Security payments are computed using your salary history and age at the time of claim. Understand the different elements that might influence your benefit amount, including your full retirement age, claiming strategy, and spouse benefits. Explore the Social Security Administration's online information and tools to estimate your anticipated benefits and make educated decisions about whether to file a claim.

I: Maximizing Your Social Security Income.

Maximizing your Social Security income necessitates careful preparation and consideration of several factors that might influence your benefit amount. Investigate techniques for maximizing your Social Security benefits, such as postponing claiming to raise your benefit amount, coordinating benefits with a spouse, or using spousal or survivor benefits.

Considering whether to collect Social Security benefits, take into account your health, life expectancy, financial demands, and other sources of retirement income. Consider the trade-offs between claiming early and obtaining decreased benefits or postponing claiming to maximize rewards in the long run. Consult a financial advisor or Social Security specialist to discuss personalized claiming tactics that are geared to your specific situation.

III: Understanding Pension Plans and Benefits.

Pension plans are employer-sponsored retirement benefits that offer a steady source of income to eligible employees in retirement. Understand how pension benefits are calculated based on years of service, income history, and other eligibility conditions set by your employer's pension plan.

Learn about the many types of pension plans, including defined benefit and defined contribution plans, as well as the differences in benefit structure, financing processes, and investment alternatives. Understand your pension benefit entitlements and alternatives, such as lump-sum payments, annuities, and survivor benefits.

Decoding Social stability and pension benefits is critical for increasing your retirement income and establishing financial stability in retirement. Understanding how these benefits function, when to claim them, and how they fit into your overall retirement plan allows you to maximize your income streams and have a happy and meaningful retirement. Remember, proactive planning and educated decision-making are essential for realizing the full potential of your Social Security and pension benefits.

Chapter 8:

Health and Long-Term Care Planning for Retirement

We will consider the critical issues of retirement health and long-term care planning, both of which are essential components of any comprehensive retirement strategy. Understanding healthcare expenditures, long-term care alternatives, and techniques for preserving health and wellbeing is critical for ensuring your financial security and quality of life in retirement.

Section 1: Understanding Healthcare Costs during Retirement

Healthcare expenses are an important concern in retirement planning, with prices changing depending on age, health condition, region, and insurance coverage. Learn about common healthcare expenses in retirement, such as premiums, deductibles, copayments, prescription medicines, and out-of-pocket spending.

Prepare a budget for medical treatment, preventative services, and unforeseen healthcare crises. Examine healthcare coverage choices, such as Medicare, supplemental insurance (Medigap), and retiree health benefits, to reduce financial risks and assure complete coverage in retirement.

II: Long-term Care Insurance Options.

Long-term care (LTC) insurance covers the services and assistance required for chronic diseases, impairments, or age-related problems that limit everyday activities. Understand how LTC insurance may safeguard assets and provide financial stability in the case of long-term care demands

Examine LTC insurance alternatives, such as classic LTC plans, hybrid LTC policies, and self-funding solutions, to choose the best coverage for your requirements and budget. Consider coverage limitations, benefit durations, elimination periods, inflation protection, and policy features when choosing a policy that meets your long-term care needs.Section

III: Strategies to Maintain Health and Wellness

Maintaining health and wellness is critical for having a joyful retirement and lowering healthcare costs. To improve physical and mental well-being in retirement, follow good lifestyle habits such as frequent exercise, balanced eating, appropriate sleep, and stress management.

Invest in preventative care, such as routine health screenings, immunisations, and preventive treatments, to detect and manage health risks early on and reduce long-term healthcare expenses.

Participate in social activities, hobbies, and community service to strengthen social connections, reduce loneliness, and improve your general quality of life in retirement.

Health and long-term care planning are critical components of a comprehensive retirement strategy and financial stability after retirement. Understanding healthcare expenses, researching long-term care insurance choices, and prioritizing health and wellbeing may help you protect your financial well-being and experience a meaningful retirement. Remember, proactive preparation and lifestyle choices are critical to sustaining health, happiness, and independence in retirement.

Chapter 9:

Estate Planning and Legacy Building.

Estate planning and legacy building, both of which are critical components of preserving your assets and ensuring your desires are carried out after you die. Understanding estate planning concepts, developing a thorough strategy, and leaving a legacy for future generations are critical steps towards gaining peace of mind and making a lasting influence.

I: The importance of estate planning.

Estate planning is the process of arranging for the administration and distribution of your assets after death or incapacity. Regardless of your age or income, estate planning is critical for safeguarding your loved ones, reducing taxes, and ensuring your intentions are carried out.

Recognise the value of estate planning in maintaining family unity, avoiding administration, and providing for dependents. Failure to develop an estate plan may result in legal problems, asset distribution conflicts, and unplanned tax implications.

II: Creating a Will and Trust

A will is a legal document that specifies your desires for the disposal of your possessions, the appointment of guardians for young children, and the appointment of an executor to handle the probate proceedings. Understand the major components of a will, including beneficiaries, bequests, and provisions for situations.

Investigate the advantages of using trusts as part of your estate plan, such as probate avoidance, asset protection, and secrecy. Learn about the many types of trusts, such as revocable living trusts, irrevocable trusts, and special needs trusts, as well as their objectives and benefits.

III: Preserving Your Legacy for Future Generations

Building a legacy extends beyond financial riches to include the beliefs, ideals, and memories you leave for future generations. Consider your legacy objectives and aspirations, including how you want to be remembered and the influence you hope to have on your family, community, and society.

Investigate methods for maintaining your legacy, such as documenting family history, passing on customs and ideals, and philanthropic giving. Consider setting up charity trusts, endowments, or foundations to help you're eager about leaving a lasting impression on the world.

Estate planning and legacy building are critical components of preserving your assets, protecting your loved ones, and leaving a lasting legacy for future generations. You may gain peace of mind and make a lasting influence by recognising the importance of estate planning, developing a thorough strategy, and building a legacy that aligns with your beliefs and objectives. Remember that estate planning is more than simply arranging for the end of life; it is also about leaving a lasting legacy.

Chapter 10:

Managing Retirement Transitions and Lifestyle Changes

In this key chapter, we look at the numerous transitions and lifestyle changes that come with retirement, leading you through the process of adjusting to this new era of life with confidence and purpose. Understanding the emotional, social, and financial components of retirement transitions is critical for successfully navigating this transforming journey and seizing the possibilities it brings.

I: Accepting Retirement Transitions.

Retirement causes a dramatic change in daily routine, identity, and purpose. Accept these shifts as chances for personal growth and discovery. Recognise the emotional effects of retirement, which may include feelings of exhilaration, uncertainty, or grief, and give yourself time to adjust to the new life.

Explore new interests, hobbies, and activities to make your retirement years more enjoyable and fulfilling. Whether you're traveling, volunteering, pursuing artistic endeavors, or spending time with loved ones, take advantage of the freedom and flexibility that retirement provides to explore new hobbies and experiences.

II: Adjusting Financial Strategies.

Retirement transitions frequently necessitate changes to financial plans to guarantee your financial stability and support your preferred lifestyle. Examine your retirement budget and spending patterns to discover areas where costs may be optimized or lowered to better fit with your income sources and retirement objectives.

Evaluate your investment portfolio in terms of risk tolerance, asset allocation, and withdrawal methods. Consider options for producing retirement income, such as annuities, systematic withdrawals, or part-time work, to augment your retirement resources and maintain your chosen level of living.

III: Prioritising Health and Wellness.

Maintaining health and fitness is essential for a good retirement. Prioritize self-care habits that promote your physical, mental, and emotional well. Incorporate regular exercise, healthy eating habits, adequate sleep, and stress-management skills into your daily routine.

Maintain optimal health by scheduling regular check-ups, screenings, and vaccines. Develop social ties and meaningful interactions with friends, family, and community members to provide a sense of belonging and support in retirement.

Managing retirement transitions and lifestyle changes needs flexibility, perseverance, and a positive outlook. You may confidently and purposefully negotiate the complexity of retirement by accepting change, modifying financial plans, and prioritizing health and wellness. Remember that retirement represents a new chapter in your life, full with opportunity for development, adventure, and fulfillment.

Chapter 11:

Accepting Purpose and Meaning in Retirement

We'll look at how finding purpose and meaning in retirement may lead to a meaningful and rewarding post-career existence. Understanding the importance of purposeful living, pursuing opportunities for personal improvement, and participating in meaningful activities are all necessary for building a purpose-driven retirement that is enjoyable and fulfilling.

I: Finding Your Retirement Purpose

Retirement is a wonderful chance to rediscover your sense of purpose and pursue new hobbies and interests. Take some time to explore what makes your life meaningful and fulfilling, taking into account your values, interests, abilities, and goals.

Investigate activities, interests, or causes that align with your beliefs and provide a feeling of meaning in your life. Volunteering, pursuing artistic endeavors, mentoring others, or acquiring new skills are all ways to engage in activities that connect with your passions and add to a sense of fulfillment in retirement.

II: Staying Engaged and Active.

Staying involved and active is critical for retaining a feeling of purpose and well-being during retirement. Keep your mind sharp and your body healthy by engaging in intellectual, social, and physical activities.

Investigate options for lifelong learning, such as taking classes, participating in discussion groups, or attending seminars on areas of interest. Cultivate social relationships by engaging in community events, joining groups or organizations, or volunteering for issues that you care about

III: Making a Lasting Legacy

Leaving a lasting legacy is an essential component of discovering purpose and meaning in retirement. Consider how your activities, ideals, and contributions may benefit your community, society, and future generations.

Consider philanthropic options, such as contributing time, resources, or skills to charity organizations or issues that are important to you. Mentor, teach, or pass on family traditions and beliefs to help others benefit from your wisdom, experiences, and life lessons.

Embracing purpose and meaning in retirement is critical to living a successful and rewarding post-career life. Discover your retirement purpose, keep involved and active, and leave a lasting legacy to build a sense of fulfillment and joy that transcends financial success. Remember that retirement is more than just leisure and relaxation; it is also about finding meaning and purpose in every stage of life.

Chapter 12:

Developing Social Connections and Relationships During Retirement

This chapter discusses the necessity of making social connections and fostering relationships in retirement. Understanding the benefits of social interaction, pursuing opportunities to make meaningful connections, and keeping solid relationships are critical for enhancing general well-being and happiness in retirement.

I: The Value of Social Connections

Maintaining mental, emotional, and physical health in retirement requires strong social relationships. According to research, having strong social networks is related with a decreased incidence of depression, higher cognitive performance, and longer lifespan

Recognise the value of maintaining contact with family, friends, and community members in retirement to overcome feelings of isolation and loneliness. Prioritize social activities and relationships that offer you happiness, laughter, and a sense of belonging in your life
.

II: Creating Meaningful Relationships

Building meaningful connections in retirement entails actively searching out chances for connection, participation, and mutual experiences. Discover new methods to meet people and form connections based on shared interests, values, and life experiences.

Join clubs, groups, or organizations that share your interests, passions, or views to broaden your social circle and meet like-minded people. Engage in community events, volunteer activities, and group trips to build meaningful relationships.

III: Developing Existing Relationships.

In retirement, it is equally crucial to nurture current relationships as it is to establish new ones. Spend time and effort sustaining intimate relationships with family members, friends, and acquaintances who improve your life and provide joy and support.

Stay in touch with loved ones through regular contact, whether it's in-person visits, phone conversations, video chats, or written letters. Make an effort to show appreciation, express thanks, and celebrate milestones together to develop friendship and love.

Building social connections and fostering relationships is critical for boosting happiness, fulfillment, and general well-being in retirement. Recognising the value of social interaction, actively developing meaningful relationships, and cultivating existing connections allows you to create a lively and supportive social network that boosts your retirement experience. Remember that the quality of your relationships is a major determinant of your happiness and satisfaction in retirement, so make wise investments.

Conclusion:

In conclusion, achieving retirement happiness requires a lifestyle that combines financial independence and personal fulfillment. We've gone over the key components of a successful retirement plan in this book, from financial tactics to emotional well-being and everything in between.

As you traverse the complexity of retirement planning, keep in mind that it is more than just acquiring cash or checking off boxes on a to-do list. It is about creating a life full of purpose, meaning, and happiness. Retirement provides unlimited opportunities for creating the life you choose, whether you want to travel the world, pursue lifetime hobbies, or just spend quality time with loved ones.

Prioritizing financial security, cultivating relationships, pursuing personal growth, and embracing new experiences can help you plan for a meaningful and joyful retirement. Remember, retirement is not the end of the journey, but rather the beginning of a new chapter packed with chances for development, discovery, and enjoyment.

As you start on this new chapter in your life, may you find the bravery to pursue your aspirations, the knowledge to manage life's twists and turns, and the strength to overcome any obstacles that arise. Here's to a retirement full of plenty, pleasure, and the ability to live your life on your terms. Cheers to your road to retired happiness!

www.ingramcontent.com/pod-product-compliance
Lightning Source LLC
Chambersburg PA
CBHW050243230526
45470CB00005B/2094